My Priceless Prayerbook

A Childhood Keepsake of Building Blocks to Faith, Values and Self-Esteem

New Thought Edition

by

STEVE VIGLIONE

Lighthouse Publications
"Guiding You To Your Greatest Good!"

The author has been very careful to respect all people everywhere. Any slights against people or organizations are completely unintentional.

Edited by Reverend Beverly Craig, Judy Rosen and Rose Cook
Typeset by Denise Doherty
Illustrations and cover art work by Becky Parish
Illustrations and cover concepts by Steve Viglione
Director of Marketing: God

Attention Churches, Social Organizations, Charities:
Quantity discounts are available on bulk purchases of this book for gift giving, fund raising or retailing. It can make a wonderful "thank you" to those who tithe and support.
Increase awareness of your organization by custom imprinting its name on our back cover. For more information call 1-800-684-1313.

ISBN 0-9645224-1-1

Manufactured in the United States of America

"My Highest Good,
is the best thing for me,
so when I pray,
that's what I see!"

This book is dedicated to my two
wonderful children, Alexia and Tyler.

It is also dedicated to all children
everywhere, that they have peace,
love and happiness in their lives.

This page is dedicated in loving
memory of my sister,
Sandra Marie Viglione,
also known as Sandy Beach.

Foreword

Even as a teenager, Steve Viglione practiced his faith on a daily basis with sincerity and openness I have seldom seen.

I have watched him grow from a singer-entertainer-bachelor to one of the most loving and caring husband-fathers I know. Regardless of what he is doing, at work or at play, he keeps the Presence of God in mind. Self-esteem issues have taught him how important words of care, love and encouragement are to a growing child.

In these prayer poems, Steve Viglione has brought a deep, strong, abiding and powerful faith to a simple level. Infants and toddlers can absorb the mood that is created, even if they cannot understand their meanings. Like seeds of a flower, they will root now and bloom later.

I only wish that all children might have the advantage of being held in their parents' or grandparents' arms, having these prayers read to them daily.

Reverend Maureen Sheckinah Christopher, R. Sc.F.

About Steve Viglione and His Books

In addition to being an author, Steve Viglione is a singer-entertainer and family man. He has successfully promoted and performed concerts in and around the New England area. Steve loves writing and running his business from home because it allows for more family time.

This book is his second published book. He states: "Spirit moved through me and created *My Priceless Prayerbook,* First Edition, which combines positive prayers with some traditional types of prayers. I wanted something for New Thought and traditional religions which is exactly what evolved in the first book. I see it as a bridge between the two."

Still, Steve knew there needed to be something specifically for New Thought, so when Reverend Beverly Craig of the International Youth and Family Ministries called him with the idea of a New Thought Edition, he was ready to deliver. "It was definitely Spirit creating again. Reverend Beverly and the United Church of Religious Science played a key role in bringing this second book to life. I am grateful to all those who contributed."

Steve has been a student of New Thought for more than eighteen years. He is a member of the Light of the World Church of Religious Science in Quincy, Massachusetts. "The people in our church provide outstanding support which is necessary in the pursuit of dreams. The sense of community is wonderful here," Steve exclaims.

His mission is to inspire, heal, energize, enlighten, and to share what he has learned to help others realize their greatest potential.

Steve's most heartfelt desire is one most of us share; harmony and peace among and between all people and nations. He believes the solution is found in the application of Universal Principles and is what we in New Thought already know: *when we love and accept ourselves, loving and accepting others comes naturally.*

How to Contact Steve Viglione

Any inquiries about the author's availability for speaking engagements and book signings should be directed to the address below or call us for more information.

Lighthouse Publications
27 South Munroe Terrace
Suite #4000
Boston, MA 02122

1-800-684-1313

A Daddy to his little girl

When I peek in your room
and find you fast asleep,
on top of your blankee,
dreaming those dreams
that little girls do,
such a feeling of warmth comes over me,
I want it to last forever.
Your love is so radiant, so pure.
Our love together is the strongest
of any bond.
You are the light of God's eyes,
shining brightly upon the world.

A Daddy to his little boy

My little boy, my son.
I see the world in your eyes.
I can see your personality
shaping you to be,
someone the world has
needed for so long.
You are a leader,
you are strength,
a reflection of God's own soul.
Why tonight you sleep
and grow in peace,
for tomorrow you will shine.

TABLE OF CONTENTS

Introduction

A child thrives on love, hugs, attention and care amongst a world of other things. What could be more beautiful than giving our children faith and values which will serve them the rest of their lives? By our example they will learn to be thankful for what they have, build faith for what is yet to come, and value themselves and others by practicing respect and kindness.

My Priceless Prayerbook is a child's building blocks to faith, values and self-esteem. Repeating prayers daily can give your child remarkable insight and strength. It is my hope that each child who hears these prayers receives these gifts. However, it is you the parent or grandparent who will spend a few minutes each day guiding them through this book.

Make it fun. Make it interesting. Have them repeat lines after you. As they grow older, have them read on their own.

To give our children a sense of spirituality and belonging is to give them a base for their individuality. By achieving these goals they are aligned with their Highest Good so they will live more abundantly, more prepared and more productive than generations past could ever have dreamed. Helping any child to follow a path illumined with light, love and peace helps shape the future of our world as the most tranquil in all its years of hosting human-kind.

That is my dream.
So it is.

In love and thanks,

Steve Viglione

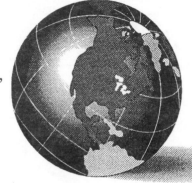

Ideas on Using This Book

This book was written for parents and grandparents to use when spending quality time with their children or grandchildren.

Enjoy your quality time!

If you only see your child at night because you work, prayer time can give you and your child a real sense of bonding. Take advantage of this time.

Say prayers together as a family.

Teach and live in an attitude of "Thanks." Look around you and see the beautiful things we have. Especially our children, they are the greatest gifts God has given us.

For this alone we can be thankful.

Put away a copy of this book for each of your children so they can share it with their kids and remember the precious moments you created for them. Write a special note in it from you.

Make it a family keepsake.

Send a copy of this book to someone who may need it.

This book makes a wonderful gift for "new" parents.

Ideas for Children as They Grow

Encourage children to say their own prayers, too. This exercise strengthens and personalizes their faith. When they're old enough, have them write and illustrate them as well. (See My Own Priceless Chapter.)

Admire your child's creativity!

Have them consistently tithe to their church or place where God means the most to them. This in itself is the very basis of "faith in action" and can give them tremendous fulfillment: spiritually, financially, physically and psychologically.

Tithing can be accomplished in the form of time, things or money.

Have your child save 10¢, 25¢, 50¢ or $1.00 per day, (See Money Wise page 55). The idea is habitual savings. Learning these skills from the very beginning helps make a difference in the way a child views his/her own competency.

Financial independence starts here.

Store duplicate photos and videos of your children in a safety deposit box or at a friend or family member's home. This increases the chances you will always have copies of these priceless valuables.

It's worth the extra effort!

It's great to have powerful faith, however, always maintain an awareness of what's around you. Always use common sense. Be vigilant in your guidance. As your children grow through the years build trust and gradually learn to let go and let God.

Allow everyone in your family to live life to the fullest.

A Priceless Gift From

This book is a gift of love from _____

_____

for _____

on _____

Here is a special message from me to you on this day:

_____

_____

_____

_____

_____

_____

_____

_____

_____

_____

_____

_____

This Priceless Book Belongs To

Name: _____

Street: _____

Town/City: _____

Zip Code: _____

Country: _____

Time I was born: _____

On: _____

At: _____

Address: _____

Weight: _____

Length: _____

"I Am Special…

…I Am Loved"

What People Are Saying About My Priceless Prayerbook:

"Steve Viglione offers a wonderful way for parents and children to spend good quality time together, while learning to love and appreciate everyone and everything in the world around them."

Louise L. Hay
Author of *You Can Heal Your Life*

"A fantastic spiritual guide for all children! It assists them in accepting themselves, others and life itself, as good and very good!"

Dr. Margaret Stortz
President, United Church of Religious Science

"Steve's sincerity and his love for children and God shine through on every page."

Dr. Alan Anderson and Dr. Deb Whitehouse
Authors of *New Thought: A Practical American Spirituality*

"What a wonderful tool to cultivate a spiritual time together and imbue your child with self-respect. Steve Viglione's prayer poems are a gift of the soul."

Marilyn Ross
About Books, Inc.
Award-winning author of ten nonfiction books.

"Children live up to or down to the expectations set before them. Steve speaks the word for all children, and God through them will do the rest. What a precious lifetime gift this book is!"

Rev. Mimi Ronnie
Executive Director, International New Thought Alliance

NEW BABY

For a New Baby

For _____'s new baby,
being born to this day,
a picture of health,
God's leading the way.

The baby's surrounded by love,
and is so secure,
whatever it needs,
God does assure.

God's miracle is happening,
life is aglow,
A wonderful moment,
in Spirit I know.

For the new baby's years,
they are filled with peace.
Now all this is done,
to God I release.
So it is. Amen.

God Has Faith in Us

A new baby
is proof God
has faith in us.
The past, present
and future are
all wrapped up
in one little
bundle of joy.
God believes
in us
every time a
baby is born.
Amen.

God Loves a Baby

God loves a baby.
Babies come from God and are
the sweetest reminder of a miracle.
We know that every one of
them is loved and well taken
care of. Amen.

MORNING PRAYERS

Morning Is Beautiful

Morning is beautiful,
hearing the birds chirp away.
Singing their favorite songs,
preparing for the day.

The animals fresh awake,
from their nightly sleep.
Cows, ducks and hens,
the frogs in the deep.

The smell of fresh air,
with the windows open wide.
For those near the ocean,
who are watching the tide.

From the beaches to the mountains,
people everywhere,
enjoying this beautiful morning,
and maybe even this prayer.
Amen.

Partners

Good morning God,
I am thankful for this day anew.
I remember we are partners,
in everything I do!
So it is. Amen.

A New Dawn

A new dawn awakens,
like a dream coming true.
The sun is rising,
turning the sky pink to blue.

The mist is lifting,
the water is still.
Nature at work,
doing God's will.

Truly a wonder,
this birth of a day,
soon my friends and I,
will be busy at play.
Amen.

Morning "To Do's"

It's time for morning "to do's,"
like washing my hands 'n face,
combing my hair,
picking up the place.

Putting my "jammies" away,
"slippies" under my bed.
Putting on clean clothes,
maybe a hat on my head.

I make this fun,
these morning "to do's,"
last but not least,
I tie my shoes.

Being Special

I wake up today
with love and peace
in my heart.
I carry them with me
wherever I go and
to whoever I see.
I know others
will feel good
when I am near.
For they'll know I am
a special person
God has made
and loves.
Somehow I make them
feel special, too.
For this I give
thanks.
Amen.

NAPTIME PRAYERS

Morning Nap

Morning games are over,
I had lots of fun.
Now I'm quiet and relaxed,
my nap time has begun.
Amen.

I Need My Nap

I need my nap,
because my body loves to rest.
It's also very good for me,
and makes me feel my best!
Amen.

Bless Me at Bedtime

I am blessed while I sleep,
Spirit's love I am to keep.
Amen.

Afternoon Nap

It's time for my afternoon nap,
to snuggle in my bed.
I fall fast asleep,
now my prayer is said.
Amen.

MEALTIME PRAYERS

What a Miracle It Is

What a miracle it is
to have this food
in front of us.
It came
from God's good earth
to this table,
to give us the *energy*
we need.
So we give thanks for
this meal as well
as the next one, too.
Amen.

A Blessing

This food
is blessed
as
it travels
through my body.
Amen.

Good Is in My Food

Good is in my food,
I bless it on my plate.
I eat the right amount,
keeping balance to my weight.

Happy Loving Thoughts

I look upon my dinner,
with happy, loving thoughts.
So it may return to me,
the energy it brought.

Giving Thanks

I give thanks
for the food we eat
and the energy
it gives us.
These are truly gifts
of Spirit.
So it is. Amen.

After Meals

God blesses the food
we just ate.
We liked it so much,
it's gone from our plate!
Amen.

My food is
perfectly and lovingly
digested.
So it is. Amen.

EVENING PRAYERS

The Stars Are Beautiful

The stars are beautiful,
a wonder of God I know.
It feels simply magical,
to sleep beneath their glow.

When in a Storm

When we are in a storm,
nature is doing Its work.
I am calm and still,
knowing God's presence
is in, around and through me.
Spirit protects me and all
those I care about. I let
go and am relaxed.
Amen.

Starry Skies

Oh starry skies above,
I'm so happy to see you.
Twinkling in the night,
making morning dew.

So beautiful,
when all is dark.
It's quite a wonder,
where you get your spark.

Oh starry skies above,
I'm so happy to see you.
Even when it's cloudy,
I know you're up there, too.

You make my night so calm,
knowing you're mine to keep.
It's you I'll be dreamin' of,
as I fall asleep.
Amen.

I Am

I am
important.
I am
special.
I am
loved.
I am
somebody.
I am
healthy.
I am
made in God's image
and likeness.
For I am
a
child of God.
Amen.

God Is Everywhere

God is over all.
God is under all.
God is through all.
Amen.

I Thank God

I thank God for our health,
our most important thing.
I thank God for our voices,
so that we can sing.

I thank God for our eyes,
so that we can see.
I thank God for love,
and caring about me.

I thank God for our ears,
so that we can hear.
I thank God for our hearts,
a place we keep love near.

I thank God for our noses,
so that we can smell,
the daisies and the roses.
These gifts God gave are swell!
Amen.

Precious Spirit

Precious Spirit, I am thankful
my prayers are answered
in the best way possible, because Spirit
knows what's best for me and those
I pray for. I now let go and let God.
So it is. Amen.

For Feeling Loved

Because God made me,
I know I am special,
and others are, too.
So I love them and myself.

I love (*name friends and family,*)
and they love me.
Amen.

Prayer for My Teddy

Right now I pray for my teddy,
who comforts me all the time.
So soft and warm and cozy,
the love we share is fine.

To treat it kind and gentle,
by a hug when the day is through.
Then I tell it goodnight, you know,
cause it has feelings, too.
Amen.

Prayer for My Dolly

For my dolly I now pray,
that she knows I love her, too.
For all the hours that we play,
for our friendship that is true.

For the good times that we share,
on a picnic or a ride,
and the fact she does care,
about how I feel inside.
Amen.

My Highest Good

My Highest Good,
is the best that can be,
for myself,
and for my family.

Wherever we are,
whatever we do,
the Good that is here,
comes shining through.

My Highest Good,
is the best thing for me,
so when I pray,
that's what I see!
So it is. Amen.

All Kinds of People

There are all kinds of people,
in this world, yours and mine,
we're different yes,
yet all made Divine.

Our skin may be different,
like a light or dark horse,
however equal in heart,
and belonging of course.

We may be tall or short,
pudgy, skinny or small.
But the whole key to life,
is loving us all.
God does. Amen.

Love Prayer

What is love?
Love is God here on earth,
a warm hug,
a pet who snuggles.

Love is my bed, my
favorite shoes, toy
or blanket.

Love is the sweet smell
of flowers and trees,
my dinner cooking,
my freshly washed clothes.

Love is being tucked in at night,
my family,
my home,
wherever it is.

Love is the sound of birds,
the wind,
the rain,
the ocean dancing its
way to shore.

Love is everywhere and everything.
It is my way of knowing that
God is in all places at once.
Always loving and keeping me
safe and warm.

For all this love,
I give thanks.
So it is. Amen.

Good Night!

Good night God.
Good night light.
Good night everyone.
Good night, good night!

ANYTIME PRAYERS

God Made

God made the sky,
and the clouds that float.
God made the ocean,
and my little toy boat.

God made the water,
for which I need.
God made the flowers,
from the soil and the seed.

God made me, too,
as well as my best friend.
God made everything,
for that I say Amen!

The Power of God's Love

The power of God's love,
is everywhere I know.
In the farmers and their corn,
a miracle they sow.

The power of God's love,
travels from shore to shore.
Supplying people everywhere,
happy to give us more!
So it is. Amen.

God Is Our Source

God is our source,
for everything we need.
Be it food or water,
clothes or books to read.

God provides for us everyday,
when I look around I see.
For this I am thankful,
and allow my Good to be!
So it is. Amen.

Money Wise

I am money wise,
as early as can be.
And watch my savings grow,
right along with me.

A fund called "Savings for Now,"
and one called "College Then."
One called "Spending Here or There,"
while the percent to God is _____.

That makes four ways,
I divide each $ dollar by.
Now that I have made this plan,
money wise am I!
Amen.

Beauty Is From Within

Beauty is from within.
Like a fountain flowing,
from just beneath my skin.

My eyes reflect the glow,
of a candle lit,
by Spirit, I know.

For there inside,
is the real source of,
the beauty I'm supplied.

So if you think I'm beautiful,
it's because you see,
my beauty from within,
God's perfect child called me.
Amen.

God Speed

God Speed is God's own time,
it could be fast or slow.
There's no way to rush it,
it's just for God to know.
Amen.

The Sun

The earth revolves around the sun,
taking the heat it gives.
Growing our plants and trees,
because of it, everyone lives.

The way its light shines in our homes,
and on people everywhere.
It makes me feel so good inside,
to know that God is here. Amen.

The Moon

I go to bed some nights,
looking at the moon so dear.
I wonder if it sees me,
so far away from there.

It's so important to our earth,
the way it steers the tide.
Moving water up the shore,
and helping it subside. Amen.

The Lighthouse

The lighthouse stands tall,
with strength and with pride.
To the sailors in the night,
its light their guide.

A symbol of hope,
for us all to see.
From the shore or the ocean,
it reminds us we're free.

The lighthouse is a friend,
who through the passage of time,
stays loyal and true,
like the best you can find.

If you are interested in preserving
lighthouses, write to:

The Lighthouse Preservation Society
P.O. Box 736
Rockport, MA 01966

United States Lighthouse Society
244 Kearney Street, 5th Floor
San Francisco, CA 94108

I Accept!

I accept love.
I accept peace.
I accept kindness.
I accept friendship.
I accept health and joy.
I accept God who loves me.
I accept having enough of everything.
I accept that I am a wonderful child of God.
I accept that I am worthy of the very best. Amen.

I Am God's Idea

I am God's idea.
My life is part of the Divine
Plan. God has placed me here
perfectly and lovingly for
reasons more than anyone
could ever know.
I am God's dream realized,
here to express what needs to be.
So I am. Amen.

SPECIAL DAYS

DECEMBER

		1	2	3	4	5
6	7	8	9	10	11	12
13	14	15	16	17	18	19
20	21	22	23	24	Christmas ✓ 25	26
27	28	29	30	31		

Eastertime

Eastertime is a good
time to remember that
I am one with God.
I just look around and
see the miracles which
happen everyday:

the beautiful flowers and trees,
the sun shining, the fresh air,
the crisp apple, the new baby
duckling in the grass,
all are reminders that God
is right here where I am
and wherever I go.
So it is. Amen.

Happy Easter!

Cute bunnies and baskets,
colored eggs and candy, too.
I love the little yellow chicks,
and the decorations we drew!

July Fourth

Happy July Fourth!
It's Independence Day!
We celebrate and thank God
for our freedom.
Amen.

God Bless America!

God bless America!
As an owner of this country,
I do my share
to preserve its beauty
by being a neat and
clean citizen.
I only use what
I need and not waste.
By doing this I
serve this land, everyone who lives here
and all future generations.
Amen.

World Independence

Let us know right now
that we are
all God's people.
Whoever and wherever we are.
Today I accept
the world
knows independence.
Amen.

Thanksgiving Day

On this Thanksgiving Day of
football games and parades,
we celebrate
with hot meals and
tasty deserts. For all
this Good I give
thanks.
Amen.

My Thanks Is Multiplied

This Thanksgiving,
I list all the things I am thankful for.
Big or small they all are important.
Also, what is it that I can give
to someone who might not have
as much? Some toys? Some food?

For giving and receiving are the same:
when I give, I receive joy
and when others give, they receive joy, too.

Whatever I have is multiplied when
I give. It's God's way of
providing for me.
In God, I always have enough.
For God is the source of everything.
So for that reason alone,
it's a very Happy Thanksgiving.
Amen.

Thanksgiving Idea

At Thanksgiving time
why not donate a turkey
and canned food to
a nearby food pantry. If
money is a problem, you
can hold a small bake sale,
sell candy or do some odd
jobs to raise the money.
Tell people why you're doing
this.They'll be glad to help.
Giving makes everyone
feel good!

What Is Christmas Really About?

I love when Christmas time is near,
it's a wonderful season of the year.
  With decorations, oh so nice,
and toys, gifts and merchandise.

But what is Christmas really
about?
The One Mind filling Jesus
and the world
throughout.

So with faith in God,
I go to sleep.
Knowing the truth
about Christmas,
is mine to keep.
Amen.

Merry Christmas

Merry Christmas
to the Christ within me.
Giving joy is my
gift to others.

New Year's Day

I am thankful
for this year past,
another one is new.
I welcome all the Good,
in store for me and you!

For Others

(Say the name of the person where the blank is)
Today is _____'s birthday
Bless and give_____health,
wealth and lots of hugs.

Over the next year I know
is guided _____
into happiness and friendships.

I know this day is a special day
for _____. I help by
wishing _____ a very
Happy Birthday!
Amen.

For Myself

On this special day,
I was born into this
world.
The most beautiful of
wonders,
like an oyster that has
pearled.

I celebrate today,
with friends and family.
My love touches them,
while their love touches me.

So, as I let my birthday be,
lots of games and fun.
Since I am center stage,
I declare this day's begun! Amen.

SEASONS' PRAYERS

Prayer for Winter

I am thankful God for winter,
for the coziness at night,
the snowflakes and the icicles,
the candles and their light.

The frost on the windows,
while cooking those hot meals.
The warmth from my blanket,
oh, how good this all feels!
Amen.

Prayer for Spring

I am thankful God for spring,
with its breath of fresh air.
To be outside again,
and feel the wind in my hair.

For the tulips and the daffodils,
yes for those I give thanks, too.
For the warmth of the sunshine,
and the sky so blue!
Amen.

Prayer for Summer

I am thankful God for summer,
these hot and playful days.
Where I enjoy my time,
in oh so many ways.

Thank you for the water,
which helps to keep us cool.
While learning how to swim,
or splashing in a pool.
Amen.

Summertime

The mountains look so wondrous,
against the summer sky.
They seem to rest so peacefully,
as the clouds roll by.

The pine trees smell so fresh,
while they stand so tall.
Behind them is the perfect scene,
the sun an orange ball.

Prayer for Fall

I am thankful God for fall,
with its cool and crispy weather.
Pumpkins, trees and falling leaves,
and yes, my favorite sweater!

The sky is growing deeper blue,
the wind is picking up.
The harvest and the full moon,
apple cider in my cup!
Amen.

The Leaves Come Down

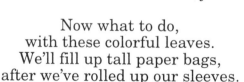

The leaves come down,
like they do every year.
We rake them up,
so the yard may be clear.

We put them in piles,
jump in them and play.
Only to rake them up again,
before the end of the day.

Now what to do,
with these colorful leaves.
We'll fill up tall paper bags,
after we've rolled up our sleeves.

PEACE AND SAFETY

What Spirit Is

Spirit is my guardian angel,
who is with me all the time.
I allow It to be present,
to bless and ease my mind.

It goes with me everywhere,
and so I trust completely,
in Spirit, Mind and Body,
God packaged me so neatly!

Prayer for Safety and Protection

I know that Spirit surrounds this home with light
and love, protecting it, guiding it
in peace.
I am calm.
I know Spirit is right
here with me,
when I'm awake and in
my dreams.
Amen.

Peace Follows Me

Peace follows me,
wherever I may go.
To the store, school or back,
it's just for me to know.

Peace follows me,
you can see it in my eyes.
It's God's living Spirit,
protecting, loving and wise.
Amen.

Peace Begins with Me

Peace begins with me.
I bring it to others,
by doing kind things.
They in turn are kind to
someone else,
and so on and so on.
So my one kind act of peace,
goes on and on and on.

When Going for a Ride

When going for a ride,
I know God to be,
in the front seat,
guiding the driver to see.

Spirit goes ahead,
making the way clear,
I do my part,
being good so we can hear.

Yes, God's love is there,
getting us where we are going.
Whether we're traveling by car,
bus, train or Boeing®.
Amen.

FAMILY AND FRIENDS

God Blesses My Family

God blesses my family,
(name all family members,)
I love them and so does Spirit.
They are a part of everything
I am and do.
I know that God
within me blesses my
family.
Amen.

For Parents or Grandparents

I am thankful to God for taking good
care of *(say their names here,)*
since they take care of me.
I know they have whatever they need
to be happy and healthy.
Amen.

For Making New Friends

I am thankful God,
for new friends that I find.
Ones that are polite,
generous, and kind.

I attract the children,
who are special just like me.
It's good quality I attract,
I deserve it certainly.

And when I play with them,
I am kind and gentle, too.
Being careful of their feelings,
making friendships that are true!
Amen.

HEALTH & GROWING

Prayer for Growing

I am thankful,
for the way I grow.
God is working in me,
loving me I know.

God gives me such wonders,
like fruits, breads and cheese.
My body breaks them down,
and says "thanks for these."

Each day I grow,
in the smallest of amounts.
Yet, after one whole year,
I see it really counts!
Amen.

Getting Well

When I feel sick,
I pray to soon get well.
It's my body's way of saying,
"we need rest, I can tell."

So, I take an oath right now,
for my health I will upkeep.
And to let God's healing power,
work through me while I sleep.
Amen.

God Heals

Say the person's name where the first blank is,
then use "him" or "her" in the blanks that follow.

Example: For Beverly I am thankful...

God within me is the source of all healing.
For _____ I am thankful
that he/she is healed in body and in mind.
I know now that _____
is completely in God's care and is
perfectly blessed,
perfectly whole,
and perfectly loved.
God is inside him/her.
I release _____ to God's healing love.
And he/she is now whole.
So it is. Amen.

A Good Idea!
Write a copy of this prayer and send it
to the person who is experiencing unwellness.

GOOD THINGS TO DO

Eating

I choose good things to eat,
because my body deserves the best.
Veggies, fruits and nuts are treats,
from the ground to me they're blessed.
Amen.

Brushing My Teeth

I choose to brush my teeth,
after each and every meal.
I know how good it is for them,
I can tell by how they feel!
Amen.

Giving

Giving is so nice to do,
it stays with me the whole day through.
Because it feels so good inside,
I do it often and I do it with pride!
Amen.

When Giving or Receiving

Divine Love, through me,
blesses all that I am,
all that I give,
and all that I receive.
Amen.

Sharing

I love to share my toys,
'cause it's the thing to do.
And when my friend shares back,
we'll have things times two!

Putting Away My Toys

Putting away my toys,
is as easy as one, two, three.
Cleaning up my room,
makes me as proud as I can be.

Washing My Hands

Washing my hands is fun to do,
using soap and water,
maybe a facecloth, too.

Before a meal or after a game,
I remember to wash,
both hands just the same!

Drinking Juice

I drink my juice,
with a smile on my face.
Made from fresh oranges,
I love how it tastes.

The best thing about it,
is it's good for me.
Sending through my body,
God's vitamin C.

I'm careful though,
when I ask for more,
to hold the cup still,
keeping my juice off the floor!

I Take Care of My Things

I take care of my things,
it's easy to do.
Putting my toys away,
keeping them like new.

I place my clothes,
where they belong.
Each time I finish,
I sing a fun song.

I Help Keep God's Earth Clean

I help keep God's earth clean,
by planting grass and trees.
This will make more fresh air,
blowing in the breeze.

I help keep God's earth clean,
by picking up the beach.
The beauty I leave behind,
is an example I like to teach.

I help keep God's earth clean,
by recycling my cans and glass.
It's not just a passing fad,
I'm just showing I have class.

I help keep God's earth clean,
by re-using items every day.
When doing all of these things,
I make it fun like play!
Amen.

It's Good to Talk

It's good to talk,
about what I'm feeling.
For if I feel badly,
it's the first step to healing.

There's no reason,
to keep things inside.
I'll tell someone who loves me,
from them I won't hide.

Those are the people who,
to all I can bare.
I can see it in their eyes,
they're listening, they care.

So brave am I,
as brave can be.
I'll be glad to share,
when you listen to me.
Amen.

Forgiveness

For those times today
that I was not behaving
my best, I forgive myself with love.
Also, I forgive Mommy
and/or Daddy for those times
they needed more patience
with me. I forgive them with love.
I know they love me more than
anything in the world.
And I love them, too. Amen.

THOSE IN
TEMPORARY NEED

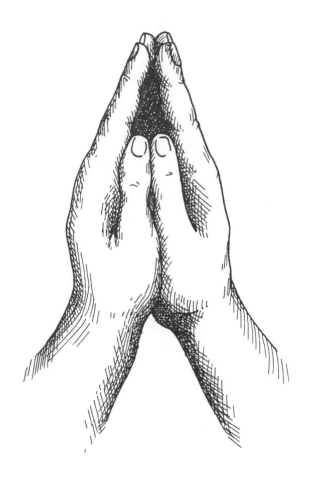

There Is Enough

There is enough of everything,
for all of us to live.
I proudly take part in this,
everytime I give.

I am thankful for your Good,
as well as I am mine.
God's gifts to us are endless,
we turn within to find.
Amen.

I Do My Part

I do my part for those,
in need of a thing or two.
I ask my Mom or Dad,
to donate clothes or shoes.

I give a toy or doll,
to a place who gives them out.
knowing I did my part
for people temporarily without.
Amen.

For Children in Other Lands

For children in other lands,
I am thankful they are fed.
That they have some clothes,
a home, a book, a bed.

God I am thankful,
for all there is to give.
For spreading it around,
so all of us can live.
So it is.

For All Children

God blesses all children,
for they are the future
of our world.
They are blessed as they grow in health
and safety.
I know they are always guided
by Spirit.
I know they are loved by God.
They now know right from wrong,
and are guided to making
good choices.
When they make a mistake it's okay.
For there is always tomorrow
and there is always forgiveness.
I know all children like me,
understand they are a part
of the One Mind.
Because we are.
Amen.

MY OWN PRICELESS CHAPTER

Lexie Vigliane

My Own Priceless Prayer

Write your own prayer here.

_____

_____

_____

_____

_____

_____

_____

_____

_____

_____

_____

_____

_____

_____

My Own Priceless Drawing

Draw your own prayer here.

My Own Priceless Prayer

My Own Priceless Drawing

My Own Priceless Prayer

My Own Priceless Drawing

My Own Priceless Prayer

_____

_____

_____

_____

_____

_____

_____

_____

_____

_____

_____

_____

_____

_____

My Own Priceless Drawing

My Own Priceless Prayer

_____

_____

_____

_____

_____

_____

_____

_____

_____

_____

_____

_____

_____

_____

My Own Priceless Drawing

Priceless Firsts

First Smile _____

First Rolled Over _____

First Sat Up _____

First Crawled _____

First Tooth _____

First Picked Up Food _____

First Stood Up Alone _____

First Step _____

First Started to Walk _____

First Word _____

First Fed Self _____

Other Notes _____

_____

_____

_____

Priceless Moments

On these pages, list those Priceless Moments
you will love to look back upon.

Priceless Moments

Priceless Moments

Thank You Pages

List here things to be thankful to God for.

_____

_____

_____

_____

_____

_____

_____

_____

_____

_____

_____

_____

_____

_____

_____

Thank You Pages

Thank You Pages

Priceless Achievements

List here your achievements which you are proudest of.

Achievement   **Date**

_____

_____

_____

_____

_____

_____

_____

_____

_____

_____

_____

_____

_____

Priceless Achievements

Achievement   **Date**

_____

_____

_____

_____

_____

_____

_____

_____

_____

_____

_____

_____

_____

Steve Viglione's
Closing Thoughts

I hope you have enjoyed *My Priceless Prayerbook, "New Thought Edition,"* and will truly use it as a guide and "childhood keepsake." I know your life is filled with love, peace, faith and strength. God bless you as you grow and learn. Know you are here to do God's work, and always remember,

**God has
a Divine
Plan
for you!**